PHOTOGRAPHY

Moira Butterfield and Susan Peach

Edited by Janet Cook

Designed by Chris Scollen

Consultant: Mervyn Maggs

Illustrated by Chris Lyon, Paddy Mounter and Kuo Kang Chen

Photographs by

Chris Gilbert, Anne Cardale and Tony McConnell.

Additional photographs by John Bellanis, Gavin Hunt, Mike Morrison, Jim Stevenson, Richard Peach, John Miles, Chris Shelton and Trevor Ball.

With thanks to Suzanne Grundy and Robert Walster

Contents

First published in 1987 by Usborne Publishing Ltd, Usborne House, 83-85 Saffron Hill, London EC1N 8RT Copyright © 1991, 1987 Usborne Publishing Ltd.

Originally published under the title Usborne Guide to Photography

Printed in Great Britain.

About this book

This book shows you how to take good pictures whatever type of camera you have. There are lots of useful tips on the secrets of setting up a good shot; for instance, by using your camera controls properly, choosing the right film, making the best of the light available and deciding where to take your picture from.

At the beginning of the book you can find out about the principles of photography and how a camera works. There is further information at the back about operating particular types of camera, such as how to load film, how to focus and how to set manual controls if you have them.

There are separate sections dealing with different types of photograph: shots of landscapes, buildings and people, action photos and pictures using flash or special lenses. There are lots of suggestions for photos that you could try and tips on creating professional effects.

A few of the photographs shown in this book are deliberately incorrect, to illustrate common mistakes that photographers make. You can recognize these by a symbol in one corner of the photo – a black cross in a small red triangle.

At the back of the book there are step-by-step instructions on developing and printing your own 35mm black and white film, and there are some tips on what to expect when you have colour photographs developed and printed professionally.

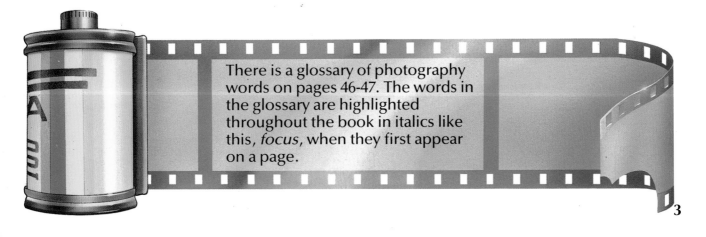

There is a glossary of photography words on pages 46-47. The words in the glossary are highlighted throughout the book in italics like this, *focus*, when they first appear on a page.

What makes a good photograph?

There are two main elements which help to make a good photograph. One of these is how technically good the picture is, for instance whether it is in *focus* or properly *developed*. You can find out how to achieve technical quality later in this book. The second element is interest. A photo may be interesting to look at for many reasons. It may be visually attractive, bring back happy memories, or it may be an unusual and striking image. There are some tips below on the elements that can make photographs interesting.

Composition

Composition is the arrangement of the things which appear in a photograph, for instance, people, objects or landscape features. Good composition helps a picture to look attractive or striking. On page 12 you can find out more about ways of achieving good composition, and avoiding common mistakes.

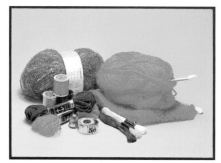

This picture is composed well – the objects are arranged in a pleasing way.

The photo above is composed badly. It is cluttered, confusing and unclear.

Atmosphere

Photographs can convey a peaceful, lively or even threatening and sinister atmosphere. This depends a lot on what you choose to put in the photo. For instance, the two pictures on the right were taken in the same general location, but they convey a completely different mood because of their content. The first one is soothing and calm; the second one looks busy and full of life.

This photo is peaceful, with no people in the picture.

This photo looks lively and active.

Dramatic, atmospheric effect

Soft, romantic light

Different lighting conditions can also affect the atmosphere of a photograph. For instance, you could take a picture with dramatic, mysterious shadows or soft, misty romantic lighting. You can find out more about coping with different lighting effects on page 10 and there are further tips on using light throughout this book.

Photographs of people

A good way to make a photograph of a person look interesting is to capture an impression of their mood or personality. You can get this effect by catching a particular expression on a face, such as happiness or thoughtfulness.

Another way of conveying someone's personality or way of life is to show them in familiar surroundings such as their home or workplace, or busy with a favourite hobby. You can find out more about taking shots of people on pages 20-25.

A happy expression

Someone busy working on a hobby.

Creating impact

Strong light and dark contrasts make this scene look dramatic.

An action shot freezing movement.

A relaxed moment caught on film.

You can make an interesting photograph by choosing a subject that will grab people's attention and make them look at it. One way to achieve this is to photograph a scene with very strong contrasts of light and shadow, as shown above.

Action shots create immediate impact by freezing a dramatic moment, such as a sporting action. Photos like the one above convey a sense of excitement and movement. You can find out more about taking action shots on page 28.

Photos of family, friends or personal events provide happy memories. The best ones often capture off-the-cuff or humorous moments. You can find out more about photographing groups of people and social events on page 24.

Professional tips

A good way to achieve successful photographs is to take lots of different views of the same subject – that way you are likely to get some that please you. Professional photographers usually take whole rolls of film of the same subject and then choose only the best photo for exhibition or sale.

Professional photographers take lots of pictures at one session.

If you have time, it is a good idea to think about what you want to convey in a finished picture before taking the photograph. Then you can decide which position to take your picture from and what to include in it for the best effect. Try to consider the lighting, the background and the composition when you are choosing your subject.

How a camera works

There are lots of different cameras available but they all work in basically the same way and have certain camera parts in common, as shown on these pages.

Principles of photography

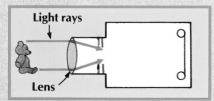

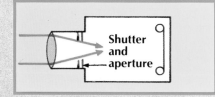

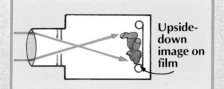

1 Light rays reflected from an object travel towards the camera. Some pass through a curved glass or plastic disc, called a *lens*. This changes the direction the rays are travelling in.

2 Camera lenses are shaped so that they direct light rays inwards. A door called a *shutter* opens to let the rays through. They also pass through a hole called the *aperture*.

3 Before they reach the *film* the light rays cross over. This means that when they hit the film at the back of the camera, they project on to it an upside-down image of the object.

Parts of a camera

All cameras have some basic features in common. These are described below.

Shutter release

When you press the shutter release button to take a photo, the shutter inside the camera opens to let light in. The amount of light it lets in depends on how long it stays open for*.

Film

To take pictures, a camera needs to be loaded with a film, usually in the back. A film has a light-sensitive coating. The type you need to buy depends on the design of your camera; the three main types are shown below. You can find out more about film on page 9 and about loading it on page 40.

Viewfinder

You look out through a camera *viewfinder* when you compose a picture. It shows you roughly the scene which will appear in the finished photo. There is more about viewfinders on page 12.

Viewfinder

Aperture

The aperture is a hole inside the camera. Its size can be adjusted to control the amount of light it lets through*. The effect of the shutter and aperture together is called *exposure*. This is a combination of how much light the film is exposed to and for how long it is exposed.

An aperture — a circle of moveable metal blades.

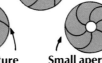

Wide aperture   **Small aperture**

Lens

A lens bends light rays so that they form an image on film. By moving the lens nearer or further from the film, the image is focused (made to look sharp)**. Lenses are described in terms of *focal length,* measured in millimetres. This figure affects the width of the scene in a photograph, called the *angle of view*. The shorter the focal length the wider the angle of view. A standard lens usually has a focal length of about 50mm.

Kinds of camera

The four most popular types of camera are shown below.

Cartridge-loading cameras

Useful for holiday or family snaps.

These cameras (called 110s or 126s) are small and compact. Some have simple manual controls and some are automatic. They may have a built-in *flash* (see page 18), and extra built-in *close-up* or *telephoto* (long distance) lenses.

Disc cameras

Useful for holiday or family snaps.

These cameras have simple exposure controls, a fixed focus and sometimes an extra close-up lens and built-in flash. Most have an autowind, to wind film on automatically after each shot.

35mm compact cameras

Useful for good quality pictures and special effects.

Some 35mm compact cameras are fully automatic. Some also have manual controls, which you can use to try out lots of special photo effects. You can sometimes buy separate lenses to fit on for special shots such as close-ups.

Single lens reflex (SLR)

Useful for good quality pictures and special effects.

These expensive cameras are named after their special "reflex" viewfinding system (see page 12). They usually have both automatic and manual controls and can be fitted with a wide range of accessories such as extra lenses.

---

*Depending on the camera this is adjusted automatically or you can do it manually (by hand) – see page 42.
For more about focussing, see page 41.   **7

Getting ready to take a picture

On these two pages you can find out how to hold and *focus* your camera, and what kind of *film* to put in it.

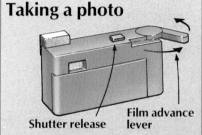

Strap round your neck or wrist in case you drop the camera.

Elbows close to your body, to help hold the camera still.

Legs slightly apart, to keep you steady.

Watch out for your fingers, hair or the camera strap getting in front of the lens.

Holding the camera

To avoid shaking the camera, which makes pictures look blurred, you should hold it firmly with both hands, as shown on the right.

Taking a photo

Shutter release

Film advance lever

It is a good idea to practise taking a photo before you load the camera with film, as this helps you get the feel of it without wasting film. On most cameras you take a photo by turning the film advance lever to wind the film on, and pressing the shutter release.*

Crouching

Sitting

Lying down

◄ You can get interesting photos by varying the position from which you take the picture, called your viewpoint. Try some of the positions shown on the left.

If you are using a heavy camera ► or an extra lens, you may need an extra support to help you steady it and avoid camera shake. Some supports you could use are shown on the right.

Rest the camera on a wall.

Lean against a wall.

Use a tripod camera stand (see page 45).

Focusing

A camera must be focused to get a sharp image. Some cameras focus automatically. Others, such as disc and 110 cameras, have a fixed focus which cannot be adjusted.

Image split in two.

This is one method, called split-image focusing.

Most cameras need to be focused manually. There are several ways of doing this, depending on your camera type. You can find out more about this on page 41.

Subject too close to the camera.

Most cameras cannot focus on subjects any closer than 1-2m (3-6ft). Your manual will give details of your camera's minimum focusing distance.

* Your camera manual will have more detailed instructions relating to your particular camera.

Film

Film is made from a transparent backing coated with silver crystals and gelatin. The silver crystals turn black when they are exposed to light, forming a *negative* image.

Different types of film have different sizes of frame (the amount of film used to take one picture). Negatives from the small frames used for 110 and disc cameras need to be enlarged a lot to make a print.

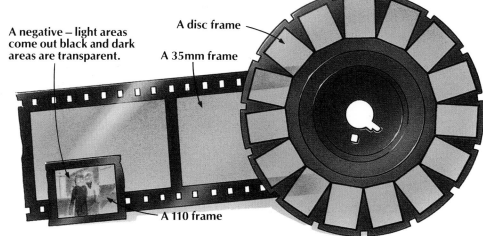

A negative – light areas come out black and dark areas are transparent.

A disc frame

A 35mm frame

A 110 frame

The more a negative has to be enlarged, the worse the quality of the print. This is why 35mm cameras, which use bigger frames and need less enlargement, produce very sharp prints.

Film speeds

Photo taken with slow film.

Photo taken with fast film.

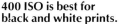

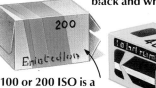

400 ISO is best for black and white prints.

100 or 200 ISO is a good general film for colour prints and slides.

Different films react to light at different speeds. Slow film reacts slowly, so you need good lighting or long *exposures.* It is coated with fine silver grains which give sharp enlargements.

Fast film is good for moving subjects or bad light because it reacts quickly to small amounts of light. It is coated with clumps of silver crystals which often produce grainy enlargements.

Cartridge and 35mm films are marked with a scale to show their speed. This is shown as an *ISO* number*. The higher the number, the faster the film. Disc film only comes in 200 ISO.

Setting the film speed

Film speed dial

DX code

When you load your camera** you normally need to set the film speed dial to the speed of the film you are using. The speed appears in a window on the dial.

Some 35mm cameras can set the correct film speed automatically. They do this by reading a pattern of metallic squares, called a *DX code,* on the film cassette.

Film for indoors

Normal film   **Tungsten film**

Photos taken with normal film under electric light bulbs look very orange. You can buy a special slide film for these conditions, called tungsten film. This gives your indoor photos a more natural effect.

* You can find out more about film speeds on page 41.
** If you do not know how to load your camera, turn to page 40.

Using light

On these pages you can find out how light affects the appearance of your photos and how to make the best use of whatever light is available.

Exposure

Letting light into the camera is called *exposure*. The amount of light that is let in is controlled by the *aperture* and the *shutter* (see pages 6-7).

A correctly ▶ exposed photo reproduces colours or black and white tones as they are in real life.

Correctly exposed photo

Overexposed photo

◀ If the aperture is too large or the shutter is open for too long, your picture will look too pale (overexposed).

If the aperture ▶ is too small or the shutter is not open long enough, your picture will look too dark (underexposed).

Underexposed photo

Electronic cell

Many cameras set the exposure automatically using an electronic cell on the front of the camera. It measures how much light there is and sets the controls. On some 35mm and *SLR* cameras you have to set the exposure. You can find out how to do this on page 42.

Lighting angles

There are three basic lighting angles – front lighting (light falling on the subject from the front), back lighting (light from behind the subject) and side lighting (light from any other angle).

Front lighting

Front lighting can be very effective for pictures of buildings and landscapes, although it tends to obscure details and make things look rather flat.

▲ **Building taken with front lighting.**

Front lighting is not ideal for portrait photos*. People squint when they are looking into the sun, and the light casts dark shadows under their eyes and nose, as shown above.

Shadow

If the sun is low in the sky, front lighting will throw your own shadow forwards into the foreground of the picture. If this happens, change your viewpoint to move the shadow.

Side lighting

Side lighting can be the most flattering angle for portrait shots like the one above. Your subject will not be squinting into the sun and the facial shadows will be more interesting *.

In landscape pictures, side lighting casts shadows which increase the appearance of perspective. It also shows up details and textures on buildings, as shown above.

Back lighting

Back lighting from a window

Back lighting can make the camera react as if it is taking a very bright photo. The subject, which has very little light falling on it, ends up underexposed, as shown above.

Sun hidden behind a tree.

If your scene is back lit but you do not want to obtain a silhouette effect, try to compose your photo so that the sun is hidden behind something. This reduces glare.

Backlighting can be used effectively for dramatic pictures, such as sunrises and sunsets. Any objects in the foreground will be silhouetted against the sky, as shown above.

Taking a silhouette

You can use back lighting to take silhouette photos, as shown here. Black and white film is best for this.

1 Sit the person in front of a light window covered with tissue or tracing paper to cut out the background.

2 Position the head carefully, so that you get the best profile.

3 Turn out the lights before you take the photo.

4 If possible, set your exposure for the background rather than the subject.*

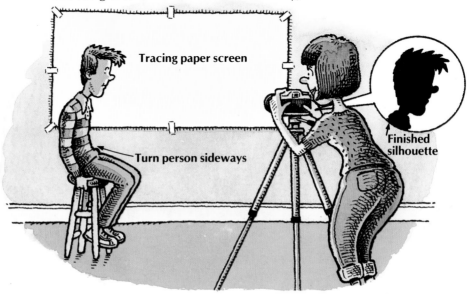

Tracing paper screen

Turn person sideways

Finished silhouette

Light at different times of the day

The light outdoors varies according to the time of day. Although the photos on the right look different, they were all taken during one day. There are strong differences in the colours, shadows and atmosphere according to the position of the sun.

You can choose which time of day you take your photo according to the atmosphere you are trying to create.

Midday – harsh light gives strong colours and short shadows.

Late afternoon – yellowish light, long shadows.

Early morning – misty, diffused light, hazy shadows.

*You can find out how to set the exposure on page 42.

Composing a photograph

On these two pages there are lots of tips on how to arrange the subject of your pictures in an interesting and effective way. This arrangement is called *composition*. You can also find out about different types of *viewfinder* below.

Using the viewfinder

A viewfinder allows you to see a scene roughly as it appears through the camera lens, so that you can compose your picture before you take it.

Most viewfinders are ▶ marked with a border frame. Only the parts of the scene inside the border frame will appear in the photo.

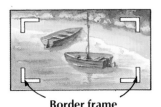

Border frame

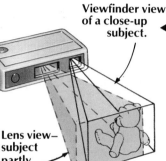

Viewfinder view of a close-up subject.

Lens view— subject partly cut out.

◀ In all cameras except *SLRs* the scene through the viewfinder differs slightly from the one through the lens. The difference between the two views is called *parallax error*. It only causes problems on *close-up* shots.

Many viewfinders have ▶ correction marks for use when the subject is less than 2m (6ft) away. These mark where the edges of the photo will be. You should position your subject inside them, as shown on the right.

Parallax correction marks.　**Subject inside the marks.**

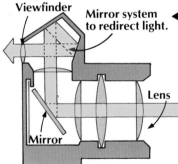

Viewfinder　**Mirror system to redirect light.**

Lens

Mirror

◀ In SLR cameras there is no parallax error because the viewfinder and the lens receive the same view. The light that comes through the lens is bounced off a "reflex" mirror system to the viewfinder.

12

Composition tips

The scarecrow is the focus of interest in this picture.

Try to compose a photo so that there is one particular object which is the main focus of interest. When people look at the finished picture their eyes will be drawn to this first, and it will give the picture interest and impact.

This picture is too cluttered, and the main subject gets lost.

Decide whether you want the focus of interest in the foreground or the background. Be careful that the background or foreground is not too cluttered, or your subject will get lost in the confusion.

The subject is positioned wrongly.

Check for background objects positioned in the wrong place. For instance, the plant looks as if it is growing out of the person's head in the photo above.

This girl looks as though she is standing on a hand.

You can get a fun effect by careful composition. The picture above was taken by standing a girl on a stool behind someone holding their hand out.

This picture looks odd because parts of people have been cut out.

Avoid cutting out parts of important objects, especially parts of people. Look at the whole scene in the viewfinder, not just your main subject. That way you will include everything you want, but cut out distracting things at the edges.

This picture has all the important parts within the frame.

If you keep finding that parts of people or objects are cut out of your photos, your viewfinder may be inaccurate. If this occurs try to work out how far the viewfinder is off-centre and compensate for this when you compose a photo.

Trying out a different camera view.

By changing your camera position you can get different views of the same objects. A new viewpoint will make a big difference to the effect of your picture. Move around and try out several views before you take a photo.

A framing device.

You can give pictures more depth by positioning something in the foreground as a frame – for instance a tree branch or an archway. This gives the effect of looking through a window to the scene that is stretching out beyond.

The road leads to the main subject.

Another way to create depth is to include lines running into the distance, such as a road or a verge. When you look at a picture your eye tends to follow the lines in it, so position your main subject at the place where the lines lead your eye.

A crooked horizon

Check in your viewfinder that your camera is straight before you take a photo, otherwise you will get a crooked image. This looks particularly odd when horizons are not straight, especially in photos of water, as shown above.

Horizontal (landscape) shots are good for wide scenes.

Vertical (portrait) shots are good for people.

When they are held normally most cameras take a horizontal-shaped picture (sometimes called landscape). You can take a vertical shot (sometimes called portrait) by turning the camera sideways.

The main subject in the middle, with lots of wasted space either side.

If you are taking a horizontal-shaped photo with one main subject, try positioning it off-centre. If you put something large and important in the middle you will get areas of wasted space on either side.

You can get more experienced at judging good composition by looking at photographs in magazines and books. Think about the way they have been composed and the effect that this has.

Taking landscape pictures

Landscapes are a popular subject to photograph, but many people are disappointed with the results they achieve.

The tips on these two pages will help you avoid the most common pitfalls and take better landscape pictures.

The same scene from different viewpoints

Choose your viewpoint

Don't just take a landscape from the first angle you see. Look at the scene from several places before you choose the best viewpoint for your photo.

General tips

Although it only shows part of the scene, this photo is very effective.

Don't just point your camera at the scene and try to fit it all in. Try to work out which is the most important and interesting aspect of the view and then concentrate on that.

The house is the focus of interest in this picture.

Try to include a focus of interest in your picture to attract the eye and give the photo impact (see page 5). This could be a human figure, a tree or a distant building, for example.

Soft evening lighting

Is your scene well lit, or would it be better to come back when the lighting is different? Early morning and evening are often the best times, as the light is soft and casts interesting shadows.

Using a polarizer

You can enhance the sky in your photos with a special *filter** called a polarizer. This reduces reflected light, and gives the sky, sea and greenery deeper colours.

Polarizing filter

The figure above emphasizes the size of the cliffs.

Large, dramatic landscapes can be more effective if you include something to give an idea of the scale, such as a human figure or a tree. This emphasizes the size of the surrounding scenery as well as providing a focus of interest for the photo.

Another way to show scale is to frame your landscape with something in the foreground, such as the overhanging branches shown above. This can also be a useful device for hiding a boring sky or any unattractive details of the scene.

*You can find out more about filters on page 27.

Overlapping photos

If you want to capture an entire landscape, try taking a series of photos. Make sure you have some overlapping areas between the photos, so that the finished pictures will fit together.

The best way to keep the photos level is to use a *tripod* (see page 45). If you don't have one you could rest the camera on any convenient support, such as a wall or post.

(see page 45)

Use the weather

Picture taken in bad weather.

Don't be put off taking landscape photos by bad weather. Overcast or rainy days give soft effects and mist or fog can veil out unwanted background details.

Landscape with a splash of colour

Photos taken in dull weather conditions look extremely effective if you include a splash of bright colour, such as someone wearing brightly coloured clothes.

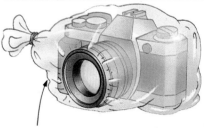

Plastic bag to keep camera dry.

Water can damage your camera, so protect it in damp weather conditions. Stay under cover, or put the camera in a plastic bag with a hole for the *lens* and, if necessary, the *viewfinder*.

Did you know?

An early photographer with his equipment.

Before film was invented, photographers used glass plates coated with chemicals which had to be *developed* and *fixed* immediately. This made outdoor photography difficult, as an enormous amount of equipment had to be carried.

Using the horizon

Try to position the horizon in your picture to emphasize the most interesting aspects of the scene.

For example, if the sky is very dramatic, a low horizon will let you include lots of it. Point your camera slightly upwards to include more sky and less foreground.

If there are important things in the foreground of your scene, point the camera slightly downwards. This will give you a high horizon and lots of foreground.

The low horizon line on this picture emphasizes the dramatic sky.

Taking pictures in the city

On these two pages there are lots of tips on how to take photos of buildings and other city scenes. You can also find out how to use a *wide-angle* lens.

Photographing buildings

Instead of taking the obvious view of a building, try looking for more unusual views. A high or low viewpoint, as shown above, will help you to get a more exciting photo.

Lots of pavement or grass in the foreground can look boring, so try to include something such as people or trees for foreground interest and to show the scale of the building.

Large buildings are often designed to dominate their surroundings. You can capture this by showing the building in its surroundings, as in the picture above.

Buildings can be rather sombre, so look for a splash of colour, such as the doorways shown above, to brighten your photo and provide a colourful focus of interest.

Parts of buildings, such as roof-tops or the windows shown above, can make good pictures. Choose a close viewpoint or use a *telephoto lens** to get a close-up shot.

Architectural details such as windows, doorways or archways often form repetitive patterns which make striking photos like the one above. Frame your subject carefully.

Making a photo montage

Pictures of buildings and architectural details make ideal subject matter for a photo montage (a picture made from several photos cut up and stuck together).

You will need a lot of prints to cut up and arrange – a series of different views of an area and its inhabitants would be ideal. You could even use a mixture of colour and black and white prints. You also need a piece of coloured card to mount the photos on.

1
Cut up interesting elements from different prints.

2
Arrange the pieces and stick them on to the coloured card.

3
To give a three-dimensional effect, mount some of the pieces on thicker card, so that they will stick out.

Street scenes

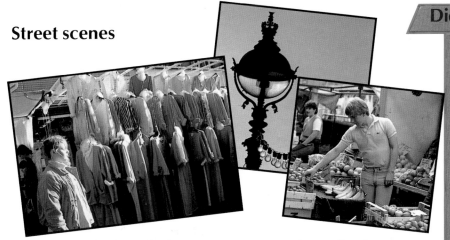

City streets offer lots of subjects for photography. Apart from the buildings themselves, you could photograph interesting street signs, market stalls, shop displays or street lamps. There are also lots of opportunities for candid shots of people.

Urban landscapes

Look out for high viewpoints which will give you views of large areas of the city. Rooftops, rows of houses, and industrial areas all make good subjects for this type of photo.

Many urban buildings, such as factories or office blocks, are quite ugly but they can still make exciting photos, particularly when contrasted with the natural environment. Try silhouetting them against the sky for a dramatic effect.

Using a wide-angle lens

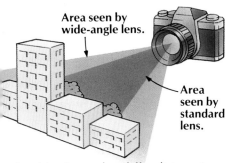

In cities it can be difficult to get far enough away from a building to fit it all in the viewfinder. If you have an *SLR* camera you can overcome this by using a wide-angle lens.

Picture taken with a wide-angle lens.

A wide-angle lens has a *focal length* of 35mm or less (see page 7). This gives a wide *angle of view* and lets you fit more of a scene into the photo without changing the viewpoint.

Distortion makes the buildings appear to lean inwards.

There are different sizes of wide-angle lens available. The more extreme lenses can see up to 180°, but they distort objects around the edges of the photo, as shown above.

17

Using flash

If you want to take photos in bad light or indoors, you will probably need to use a *flash*. There are two main types – flash bulbs or electronic flash. On these pages you can find out how and when to use flash and how to avoid common mistakes.

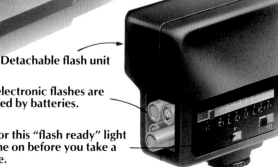

Built-in electronic flash

An electronic cell sets the right amount of flash according to how far away the subject is.

Flash cube

Detachable flash unit

Most electronic flashes are powered by batteries.

Wait for this "flash ready" light to come on before you take a picture.

A flash unit plugs in with a lead, or fits into a clip on the camera called a "hot shoe".

There are several types of flash bulbs, such as the flash cube and flipflash shown here. Flash bulbs are expensive if you take a lot of photos, as you can only use each bulb once.

Some detachable flash units have to be set by hand – your manual will tell you how.

Flipflash

When to use flash

This subject was too far away.

Flash light is very bright, but it gets dimmer rapidly the further you are away from it. Any subject more than about 3m (10ft) away will not benefit much from the flash.

This subject was too close for flash.

Anything closer than 1m (4ft) is likely to be bleached out by the intensity of the light. Flash is therefore best for subjects in a range of about 1-3m (4-10ft) from the camera.

Correct distance for flash

This range makes flash ideal for photos indoors. Flash light is very like daylight, so you can use it with your normal film and get a natural effect, even under electric lighting.

Common mistakes with flash

Some figures in this group are too light and some too dark. This is because they are at different distances from the camera and some figures are out of the flash range.

Solution: Keep all subjects the same distance from the camera and within flash range.

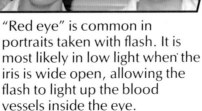

"Red eye" is common in portraits taken with flash. It is most likely in low light when the iris is wide open, allowing the flash to light up the blood vessels inside the eye.

Solution: turn on the lights and ask your subject not to look straight into the camera.

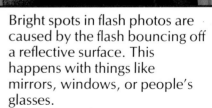

Bright spots in flash photos are caused by the flash bouncing off a reflective surface. This happens with things like mirrors, windows, or people's glasses.

Solution: choose a viewpoint where you are not directly facing a reflective surface.

Softening flash

Direct flash   **Softened flash**

Direct flash light tends to be rather harsh and throws strong shadows, which are not very flattering in portraits. The light can be softened by bouncing or *diffusing* it.

Flash bounces off ceiling on to subject.

Bouncing flash means directing the flash at a light-coloured wall or ceiling so that it will bounce on to the subject. You need a separate flash unit or one with a tilting head.

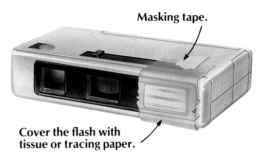

Masking tape.

Cover the flash with tissue or tracing paper.

Diffusing is a good way of softening built-in or non-adjustable flash units. You can buy a diffuser attachment, or you can make your own as shown above.

Flash outdoors

Fill-in flash dispels outdoor shadows.

Flash is also useful outdoors for portrait shots. If the sun casts strong shadows or your subject is back lit*, you can use *"fill-in"* flash to throw extra light on to their face.

Photo taken with fill-in flash.

Fill-in flash needs to be quite gentle, so that it does not create an unnatural effect. Soften your flash with a diffuser or by holding a white handkerchief over the flash.

Did you know?

Flash was first invented in the 1880s. Photographers used a tray full of magnesium powder, which they would ignite with a flint to produce a flash.

*See page 11 for more about back lighting.

Portrait photography

When you take photos of a person you can alter the pose, lighting and the background to get many different effects. For instance, you can convey a particular mood, or try to portray someone's personality by capturing a characteristic facial expression, or a fleeting unposed moment. The next few pages will show you how to take good portrait shots.

Keeping it natural

People should look relaxed and natural in portrait photos. The tips below will help you to achieve this.

★Sit your subject ▶ in a comfortable chair and let them choose a natural sitting position, so that they will look more relaxed.

◀★Photograph people in places that they know, for instance in their home or garden. This will help them relax and feel more comfortable.

★You could ask ▶ your subject to do something, such as read a book or work on a hobby. That way they will forget about the camera.

◀★Talk to your subject. This will make them feel less awkward and they will laugh or smile naturally. This will look attractive in a photo.

★Take more than one photo. As they get used to a camera people look more relaxed.

Using the background

Distracting background **Shadow cast on background**

Try to avoid strongly distracting colours and details behind your subject. Watch out for background shadow, especially if you use *flash*. Position someone 2-3m (7ft) in front of the background to avoid this.

Light background **Dark background**

If a background is much lighter or darker than your subject, an automatic camera may set the right *exposure* for the background, but under or overexpose the subject, as shown above. There is advice on this on page 42.

Depth of field

Picture taken with a small aperture. The depth of field is great – most of the picture is in focus.

Picture taken with a large aperture. The depth of field is small – only the front part of the picture is in focus.

When you *focus* on a subject there is an area in front and behind it, called the *depth of field,* which will also appear in focus. On automatic cameras with standard *lenses,* the depth of field is large, so most of the picture will be in focus.

If you have controls to alter the *aperture* on your camera* you can reduce the depth of field by increasing the size of the aperture, so that the background in a picture becomes blurred. This is useful for portrait shots.

Avoiding camera shake

When taking indoor shots without flash you may need a slow shutter speed* to cope with the small amount of light. If the setting goes below 1/60 you need to mount your camera firmly to avoid camera shake.

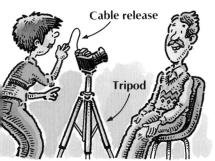

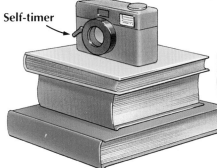

Telephoto lenses

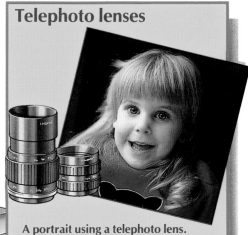

A portrait using a telephoto lens.

You could mount your camera on a *tripod* and attach a *cable release*. This allows you to take a photo without pushing down on the camera and jerking it. You can set the camera up, walk away, and then press the cable release mechanism.

Another way to keep your camera firm is to perch it on a pile of books. If you have a *self-timer* use it to avoid jerking the camera. Cock the self-timer lever and then move away. The shutter will click in about ten seconds.

Telephoto lenses are useful for portrait shots. They make things appear closer than they really are, so that you can stand further away from your subject when you use them. They are flattering to faces, too. 110 cameras often have built-in telephoto lenses. You can buy separate ones for SLR cameras.

Choosing a viewpoint

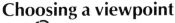

You need to stand at least 1m (3ft) away from your subject. If you come too close the final photo will show unflattering distortions. Always focus on the eyes of the subject.

You could take a vertical-shaped portrait of someone to cut out background. Or you could take a horizontal shape and use extra props to fill the space, as shown above.

People's faces appear different from varying angles. Take lots of shots from different viewpoints, or move around your subject and choose the angle you think is most flattering.

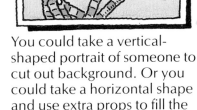

You can use camera angles to play down people's features. For instance, to lessen a double chin use a higher viewpoint. To disguise baldness point your camera upwards.

Get down to the same level as a baby or small child. If you take photos of them from above they will appear shorter than normal. If you take photos of people from below they appear taller.

In a frontal shot of someone sitting down, try to avoid including their knees. These will be closer to the camera than the rest of the body and will look unnaturally large.

Using light

Lighting plays a vital part in portrait photography. Depending on the direction of the light it can create a variety of shadows or highlights on someone's face. These variations can affect the photograph in different ways, as shown on the right.

▲ Light from one side   ▲ Face lit from the front   ▲ Light from underneath

You can soften window light by putting up net curtains or tracing paper.

Natural light is most flattering for portrait shots. Use it indoors by positioning the person near a window, sideways on. Don't pose your subject between you and the window as this will make them appear very dark.

If someone stands sideways-on to the light source half their face will be in shadow. You can overcome this by bouncing light back on to the side in shadow, using a piece of white card positioned near the face.

Reflector

Light

The white card acts as a "reflector", giving a subtle natural lighting effect. Get someone to hold it, or prop it up on a table near the subject's face, but make sure it does not appear in the finished photo.

Reflector used outside

Electric light

For outdoor portraits avoid strong overhead sun, which creates ugly facial shadows. Instead take shots in light shadow. You could use a reflector for a natural effect.

If you take an indoor picture lit with ordinary electric lighting, and you use a normal colour *film* without a *flash*, the photo will come out with an overall orange glow.

This can give a pleasing impression of warmth, as shown above. To avoid it you need to use special tungsten slide film (see page 9), or a flash.

Candid shots

Try taking shots of people when they are relaxed, and have not noticed the camera. You could *focus* on them in advance and then wait for a good moment.

You could also try including some background to portray people in their own environment, perhaps busy at their work or in their home.

Shots of people unaware of the camera.

Black and white

Black and white film gives interesting contrasts of light and shadow in portraits, and enables you to experiment with ordinary indoor lighting.

Portrait projects

Here are some suggestions for taking fun portrait photos.

1 You can create an unusual portrait by photographing a face through frosted glass. Mirror reflections also make interesting shots.

A photo through frosted glass

2 To get a soft blurry effect smear a piece of clear glass or acetate with clear gel. Hold it up close to your camera lens to take a shot*. You could try hair gel for this.

Photo through greased acetate

3 Try putting a neutral-coloured stocking over your camera, and pulling it tight so that it is close to the *lens*. This gives a soft-focus effect.

Soft-focus effect

4 Take a shot of someone hanging upside down, for instance on a park swing, with a plain background behind their head. Turn the photo round.

Upside-down shot turned around.

Funny faces

To make the picture below, take lots of photos of your family or friends and get each person to make several different faces. Cut all the photos to the size you want and then mount them on card.

Never smear the camera lens itself with grease, because you will never get it all off.

Studio secrets

Some professional portrait tricks are show below.

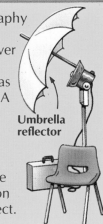

In photography studios, a white or silver umbrella is often used as a reflector. A bulb shines into the umbrella, which bounces the light back on to the subject.

Umbrella reflector

For fashion portraits, exaggerated make-up is used. Subtle lighting and filters make the effect look more natural.

Professionals often retouch prints or negatives by hand, using special dyes and inks. Using this technique it is possible to paint out unflattering shadows and blemishes.

Group photography

On these pages there are lots of tips on taking photographs of groups of people.

Large groups

To take a formal picture of a large group of people, such as a sports team or a school class, you need to arrange everyone so that their faces appear clearly on the photo.

This is often done by arranging the group in three rows, as shown on the right. You need a row of chairs, and you could also use a low bench. Alternatively, you could stand three rows of people on a slope.

Put the tallest people at the back.

Third row standing up.

Second row on chairs

Front row on the ground or low bench

Put the smallest people at the front.

Objects in the front at the centre

Small groups

◀ If you are photographing a smaller group, perhaps your family or friends, you don't have to position them very formally, but try to arrange people so that their heads are at different levels. This gives a more interesting composition. Fill the photo with the people, to cut out unnecessary background.

Using a self-timer

If you have a *self-timer* on your ▶ camera you can use it to include yourself in a group picture. When you set up the shot, decide where you are going to position yourself in the group.

Operate the self-timer, usually by pushing down a lever on the front of the camera. You will have about ten seconds to position yourself before the *shutter* clicks.

Leave a space for yourself when arranging the group.

Extra tips

★For formal group photographs, fix your camera firmly on a tripod or rest it on some other support such as a pile of books (see page 21). You can then rearrange people to get the composition you want, without moving the camera.

★Avoid lighting the group directly from the side, as this will put some people's faces in strong shadow. Also avoid strong overhead sunlight, because it will make people squint.

★Get everyone's attention on the camera by calling or talking to them, or using a signal such as whistling. While you have got everyone together take more than one shot, in order to have a choice of the one you like best.

Special occasions

Try to anticipate interesting moments at an occasion. For instance, at a wedding you could position yourself to photograph the couple as they leave the ceremony.

Look out for unique shots that others might miss. If there is an official photographer arranging formal groups, take your photos of the group members relaxing after the session.

You may not have much time to think about composition, but try to avoid cutting parts of people's bodies off the picture or including unwanted hands and heads.

You can quickly improvise a soft focus effect for special occasions by focusing and then breathing gently on your camera *lens* to mist it over. Take the photo quickly.

At a dark indoor occasion such as a wedding you may need a *flash* (see page 18). If you cannot use one, you will need to load your camera with a fast *film* to get any good results.

Don't spend too much time on your photography and end up spoiling your enjoyment. Leave official photographs to a professional, so you need not worry about getting it wrong.

People projects

Photos overlapping in a line.

Arrange friends or family into a long row and take photos of sections of the line, making sure you don't miss anyone. You could get yourself in the last photo by using a self-timer. Overlap the printed pictures to fit together.

To take the picture above ask everyone to lie on the floor with their heads close together, looking up at the camera. Or put the camera on the floor, and set it on a self-timer. Ask everyone to crowd around it, looking down into the lens.

Did you know?

Probably the world's longest photo was taken in the town of Obihiro in Japan. 1,284 town residents sat on a long line of benches. 100 cameras were placed every 4m (13ft) along the line, and they were all operated at once. The photographs were then enlarged to life size and fitted together for display.

Difficult lighting conditions

Below you can find out how to deal with difficult lighting, and how to use *filters* to enhance your photos.

Bright light

In bright conditions the main problem is the intensity of the light, much of which is reflected up off pale surfaces such as sand, water or snow.

Photos taken in bright lighting conditions.

In very bright conditions it is a good idea to choose a slow *film* (about 100 *ISO*), and to use a polarizing filter (see page 14) to reduce reflected light and give deeper colours.

Beach photos

Harsh shadows at midday

The intense light on a beach casts very strong shadows, especially at midday. The best time for photos is early morning or late afternoon when the shadows are not so harsh.

Underexposed subject

Bright backgrounds like water often fool the camera. It may treat the subject itself as very bright and underexpose it. You can find out how to overcome this on page 42.

Keep your camera in a waterproof bag, out of the sun.

Protect your camera on the beach. Keep it away from sand and water and do not leave it lying in the sun as this can damage the film. Always load film in the shade.

Lens hoods

Lens hood

A lens hood is used to shield the lens from glare. This is very useful in bright conditions. The best hoods are collapsible ones, which you can push flat when they are not needed.

Snow photos

Picture taken without a UV filter.

Snow often has a blue tinge in pictures, caused by reflected ultra violet (UV) light. You can use a special UV filter to screen out reflected light and make snow look white.

This snow scene is lit from the side.

Front lighting often makes snow look rather dull and flat. Side or back lighting is much more effective as it casts shadows which show up the contours of the snow.

Night-time photography

You cannot use *flash* for night-time photos like the ones shown below, as the subjects are too far away. Instead, use a fast film (about 400 ISO) to cope with the low light levels. You will also need a long *exposure* to let in as much light as possible.

Night-time pictures ▶ which include bright lights can be taken with any camera. A good time to take these photos is at dusk, when the dark blue sky gives the impression of night, but there is enough light left to record foreground details.

Street lights and neon signs make ideal night-time photos.

◀ On a manual camera you can set very slow exposures, which let you take a wider range of night shots. Many manual cameras have a B setting on the shutter speed dial for night-time shots. It holds the shutter open as long as the release button is pressed.

This picture of fireworks needed an exposure of several seconds.

Sunsets

Your sunset photos will look more exciting if you include some foreground interest which will be effective in silhouette, such as a tree, an interesting skyline or water, which will mirror the sky. A *telephoto* lens is useful, as it lets you zoom in on the sunset to fill the photo.

Using filters

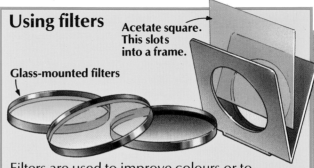

Acetate square. This slots into a frame.

Glass-mounted filters

Filters are used to improve colours or to achieve special effects. There are two main types of filters, shown above, for 35mm and *SLR* cameras. Filters reduce the amount of light coming into the camera. On manual cameras other than SLRs, you must open the *aperture* wider to let more light in*.

Acetate filter

Ready-made filters are not available for disc, 110 or compact 35mm cameras, but you can get the same effects by taping an acetate square over the lens, as shown above.

| **Starburst filter** | **Multiple image filter** |

Colour-improving filters, such as polarizers or UV filters, are used to reduce haze and make colours look richer. Pictures like the ones above are achieved with special effect filters.

Red filter used with black and white film. **Red filter used with colour film.**

Special filters are available for black and white film. These come in bright colours such as red and green, and are used to increase contrast. You can also use them with colour film for some dramatic effects.

The manufacturer's instructions will tell you how many stops to open the aperture.

Action shots

There are two ways of creating a fast-movement action photo. You can either freeze the action or deliberately blur a picture to create streaks suggesting movement. You can find out about these techniques below.

Freezing movement

To freeze action you need to use fast *film* and fast *shutter* speeds. On manual cameras the faster the action, the faster the shutter speed you need to set (see page 43 for a speed chart).* With an automatic camera try to ensure a fast shutter speed by taking shots in bright light.

Viewpoint

Action coming towards the camera.

Subjects moving sideways-on are not easy to freeze because they appear to move quite fast. You can capture a moment of action more easily if the subject is coming towards you or moving away from you.

Flash

A flash shot freezing movement.

Use *flash* to freeze quick movements in dark lighting conditions, for instance in an indoor sports hall. But remember that you can only use flash on subjects within a few metres distance (see page 18).

Peak of action

Action stops momentarily.

Some movements have a "peak of action", where everything stops momentarily, for instance at the top of an upward leap. To capture this, pre-focus** on the place where the peak will occur, and wait for the right moment.

Panning

Panning is another way of freezing movement. It means swinging the camera round to keep a moving subject in the viewfinder, and taking a shot as you move. On a panned photo the background will appear as blurred streaks, giving an idea of speed.

1 Hold the camera firmly by tucking your elbows into the sides of your body. Pre-focus on the point where you intend to take the picture. It helps to choose a point which has a clear landmark.

2 As the subject moves across your line of vision keep it in camera view by swinging around smoothly from the waist. Take a photo when it reaches the pre-focused point. Continue moving to follow the subject through.

A panned shot

Take shot here.

Pre-focused point

Move smoothly round.

28   *You can find how to set shutter speed manually on page 42.
       **If you have an autofocus camera use the focus lock – see page 41.*

Using blur

There are two ways to create blur, shown right. You need a slow shutter speed (about 1/30 on manual cameras). Hold your camera firmly or mount it on a *tripod*. If your camera has automatic *exposure,* do not use a fast film and try to reduce the shutter speed by taking pictures in overcast conditions.

1   You can move your camera deliberately to create blur. Focus on the main subject. Then, as you press the shutter, move the camera smoothly and quickly away to create blurry streaks. If you have a zoom lens you can move the camera lens in or out as you take a photo, to get the effect shown on the right.

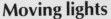

2   You can also create blur by keeping your camera steady and taking a shot of something crossing your field of vision. Focus the camera on the background, and press the shutter as the subject moves across the frame. The background will come out clearly and the moving subject will be blurred.

Professional secrets

Professionals use sophisticated equipment to get stunning action shots. Some of their techniques are shown below.

The picture above is done in darkness using a lamp called a stroboscope, which flashes on and off several times a second. The camera is set on a very slow shutter speed to capture in one photo several phases of movement illuminated by the lamp flashes.

Sports photographers often use very fast *motor drives** to take a rapid series of pictures showing a complete action sequence. The camera winds on automatically as long as the shutter button is pressed down. If you have a camera with an autowind you could try this.

Moving lights

Moving car headlights

If you can adjust the exposure on your camera you can get some dramatic night-time pictures of moving lights. Car headlights, for example, will create bright lines if you use very long exposures**. Or you could focus on stationary lights and then move your camera to get a streaked effect. In both cases you will need to use a fast film such as a 400 *ISO*

*You can find out more about these on page 45.
**On page 43 there is a chart for manual cameras showing shutter speed settings for night shots.

Close-up photos

There are some tips below for close-up photos. To take a photo less than 1m (3ft) away you need a *close-up lens*.

Close-up focussing

Cable release

Tripod

◀ The smallest camera shake will show up as blur on a very close-up picture. To avoid this, use a *tripod* or other support plus a *self-timer* mechanism or *cable release* (see page 21).

Photos using a close- ▶ up lens have a very small *depth of field*; only a limited part will come out in *focus* (see page 20). Always use the precise focusing distance recommended.

A narrow depth of field – only the front is in focus.

Lens aligned with subject.

Ruler

◀ On non-*SLR* cameras *parallax error* becomes very obvious on close-up shots (see page 12). To overcome this, look down at the camera to see if the *lens* is aligned with the subject. Use a ruler to help you.

Equipment

Close-up lenses can be screwed on to the front of some cameras. Their strength of magnification is measured in dioptres, such as +1, +2 and +3 dioptres. The higher the dioptre number, the stronger the lens. Some 110 and disc cameras have built-in close-up lenses, of weak magnification.

◀ *Macro lenses* can be fitted to cameras with detachable lenses. They can focus closer than ordinary close-up lenses, but can also be used for normal photography.

Macro lens

A *bellows unit* works in the ▶ same way as an extension tube. The bellows can be moved back or forward to vary the focusing distance.

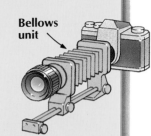

Bellows unit

◀ *Extension tubes* can be used on cameras with detachable ordinary lenses. They fit between the lens and the camera body, to vary the focusing distance of the lens.

Extension tube

All the equipment above requires special adjustments to exposure if you have a manual camera. Check manufacturer's instructions.

Flower close-ups

Windshield

A flower can easily move in the breeze and blur a close-up shot. You could protect it by setting up a piece of card nearby as a windshield. But make sure this does not appear in the finished picture.

Animal close-ups

To photograph wild animals, study their behaviour patterns so that you know when and where they are likely to appear. Stand some distance away and use a long telephoto lens to magnify the image*.

Ordinary lenses

You can get interesting close-up type pictures without using a close-up lens, by photographing detail. Get as close as your camera can focus and fill the picture frame with the detail, as shown above.

Still-life photos

In still-life photography you can experiment with shapes, colours, lighting and background, using simple everyday objects.

Still-life based on a food theme.

Layout and lighting

Arrange the objects you choose for an attractive effect. You could base your photo on a theme, for instance a hobby, as shown in the photo on the right.

Head-on lighting* accentuates reflections on shiny objects. Side-lighting creates shadows to highlight shape. To soften the effect put a screen of tracing paper in front of the light source, as shown above.

If you want a plain unobtrusive background, place things on a roll of uncreased paper, in a colour which tones well with the objects you choose. Raise the paper up behind the arrangement.

You could base your picture on warm colour tones such as red and brown, or colder tones such as blue or green, as shown above. You could also try contrasting colours – green with red, or yellow with blue.

Still-life suggestions

You can create a textured look by stretching thin cheesecloth or netting a few centimetres in front of your subject. Focus on the subject through the cloth.

You can get an attractive pattern of light bands to fall across a still-life subject by positioning it in a room near a partly-opened venetian blind.

Professional secrets

Professional food photographers often use cosmetic tricks to falsify the appearance of food in still-life photos. For instance, colour dye is used to make food appear more appetising, and water is sprayed on things to make them look very fresh. In the picture above the vegetable skins have been coated with oil to make them shiny.

*You need to use tungsten film for indoor electric lighting – see page 9.

Home developing

Film needs to be *developed* to produce *negatives,* which can then be made into prints (see page 34). You can develop 35mm black and white film* in a *darkroom* – a room which can be made light-tight. Work over a table in the darkroom, in case you drop something.

Equipment

The equipment and chemicals needed are listed below. Use liquid rather than powder chemicals as they are easier to mix up.

Developer. This brings out the negative image on a film. Mix up enough developer with water to process one film at a time. After you have used it pour it away.

Stop-bath and fixer. The *stop-bath* neutralizes developer on the negatives. The *fixer* dissolves any undeveloped silver particles on the film. Both chemicals need to be mixed with water and the solutions can be re-used. Store them for the recommended time in clean, labelled bottles.

Wetting agent. This is used when the developed film is washed. It prevents droplets of water marking the negatives. You can buy it or use a drop of washing up liquid as a substitute.

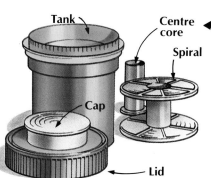

Processing tank. A light-tight plastic container with a centre core, a secure lid, a sealing cap which fits over an opening in the lid, and a spiral which holds the film inside the tank. The tank parts need to be clean and dry before use.

Measuring cylinders. ▶ Make sure these are clean before use.

Measurers

◀ **Thermometer, scissors, film clips or pegs, timer or watch with second hand.**

Optional extras – **chemical stirring rod, film opener or coin.**

Developing steps

Arrange your equipment so that you can find it in the dark. You need the tank parts, the scissors, the film cassette, plus an opener or coin. Practise loading an old film on to the spiral in daylight (see step 3), to get the hang of it. Now block out all light. Cover the darkroom windows with card held by tape.

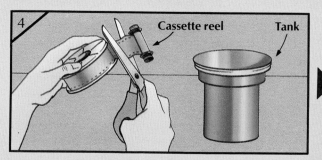

When you reach the end of the film, cut it off the cassette reel, and wind the last few centimetres in. Fit the spiral over the centre core in the developing tank, pushing it all the way down inside. Put the lid on firmly. Now you can work in daylight and mix up the developer, stop-bath and fixer.

You need to rotate the tank a few times during development (see maker's instructions). This spreads the developer evenly. When the recommended time.is up, pour the developer away and pour the stop-bath solution into the tank. Time it for the recommended period, rotating the tank a few times.

Cassette and disc films cannot be developed at home.

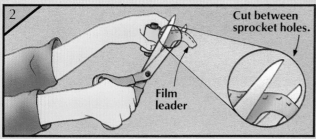

Put the light out and lever open your film cassette with the opener or coin, or by tapping it on a table. Slide the film spool out, holding it by its edges. Cut off the film leader (the shaped tongue on the end of the film). Make the cut between two film sprocket holes, as this makes it easier to load on the spiral.

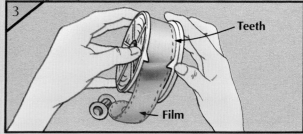

Load the film on to the spiral. The teeth on either side of the spiral should be lined up and pointing towards you, as shown above. Feed some film under the teeth. Then rotate the sides of the spiral back and forth to wind the rest of it in. If the film gets stuck or bent, take it off and begin again, holding the spiral over a table at all times.

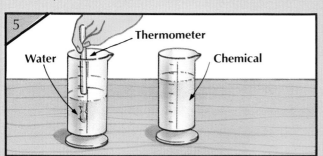

Working over a sink, dilute each of the chemicals with water to the exact measurements recommended by the makers. You need to use water of the correct temperature (see maker's recommendations). Measure this before you mix it with the chemicals. Check the temperature again after mixing.

If the solutions are cooler than the maker's recommendations, stand the containers in a tray of warm water to heat them up. At the correct temperature pour the developer into the opening on top of the tank. Start timing it for the recommended period. Fit the sealing cap firmly on to the tank.

Pour the stop-bath solution out into a storage bottle, and replace it with the fixing solution. Time this, rotating the tank a few times. Then pour the fixer out, too. Open the tank lid and wash the spiral under running water for ten minutes. Finally, fill the tank with water and add a drop of wetting solution. Soak, then pour away.

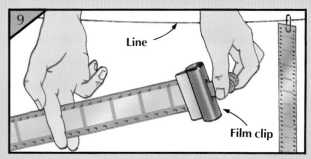

Pull the film out of the spiral and attach a film clip or peg to the end. Hang the film from a hook or line about 2m (7ft) off the ground, in a clean, dust-free place. Run clean fingers down the length of the film to remove excess water. Attach a clip or peg to the bottom of the film to weigh it down and leave it to dry.

Home printing

If you have access to a *darkroom* you can produce prints from 35mm black and white *negatives* by following the steps on the right. *Printing* involves projecting the image of a negative on to light-sensitive photographic paper. The paper is then *developed* to make the image appear. Then it is fixed, washed and dried.

Equipment

For printing you need the equipment below. You can often buy this second-hand.

Developer, stop-bath and **fixer** (see page 32). **Three processing dishes**. **Two pairs of tongs.** **Measuring cylinders, timer** and **thermometer, black card.** **Photographic paper** (see below).

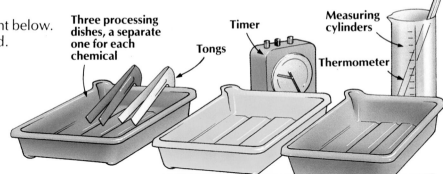

Three processing dishes, a separate one for each chemical

Tongs

Timer

Measuring cylinders

Thermometer

Safelight. A *safelight* provides enough light in a darkroom to enable you to see what you are doing. Photographic paper is sensitive to ordinary white light, but not to the safelight, which is usually red or orange in colour. You can buy a complete safelight or a safelight bulb, which will fit into a light socket.

Enlarger. An *enlarger* projects an enlarged image of a negative down on to photographic paper. You can *focus* the picture and vary the *exposure* time necessary for a print; the larger the *aperture* the less time needed for exposure. Exposure times vary depending on the darkness of a negative. You can find the best exposure time for your print by making a test strip (step 4).

A built-in red filter can be slid over the lens so that you can work with the enlarger in safelight until you are ready to make an exposure.

Baseboard and frame. Underneath the enlarger you need a baseboard to put paper on. You also need an adjustable frame to hold the paper steady.

Enlarger head. You can move it up or down its column to change the size of the image.

Negative holder

Red filter

Lens

Focusing knob

Baseboard

Frame

Photographic paper

Photographic paper is coated with light-sensitive emulsion. Always work with it in safelight until you are ready to expose it. You can buy either fibre-based or resin-coated paper. Resin-coated paper has a much shorter processing time. Both types are sold in a selection of sizes, finishes and grades.

Different grades of paper provide different levels of contrast between dark and light areas of a print. Grade 1 provides low contrast, and Grade 2 provides normal contrast. Grades 3, 4 and 5 provide progressively higher contrasts. You can choose the grade you want for a particular print, or use multigrade paper with a set of multigrade filters. These fit on to an enlarger to produce the effects of paper grades 1 to 5.

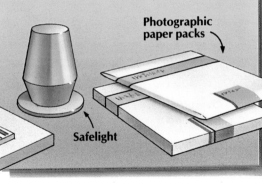

Photographic paper packs

Safelight

Mineral & Fossil Identification

AGATE a type of quartz that has hidden or microscopic crystals, and bands of color forming a circular pattern. Sometimes the agate is sliced into thin slabs or polished.

AMAZONITE a green striped or spotted variety of microline feldspar. Feldspar, 5 times as common as quartz, is found in nearly all igneous rocks.

AMETHYST is quartz crystal with colors ranging from pale lavender to deep purple. It is used mainly for decoration, and can be tumbled.

AVENTURINE is a green stone sometimes mistaken for jade. It is a type of quartz with crystals so small they cannot be seen by the naked eye.

CALCITE is a sedimentary mineral and the main component of limestone. It is found in many colors, like red, orange, green, honey and blue.

CHALCOPYRITE is a rough metallic mineral commonly called Peacock Pyrite because of its iridescent colors.

CHRYSOCOLLA is a mineral with veins of blue-green color found throughout the southwest United States, Mexico and Peru.

CITRINE is a type of quartz with brownish-yellow colors. Because of its similar appearance, it is sometimes called false topaz.

COLORED STONES may be Mexican Crazy Lace Agate which has a lacy effect from layers of minerals or Granite (black spots) which is one of the most common rocks on the Earth's surface.

COPPER is one of the 103 elements that make up all matter. It conducts heat and electricity and is essential for almost all electrical uses.

DINOSAUR BONE fragments become available as long-buried bones become exposed by the elements. These reptiles dominated the land for over 140 million years.

EMMA EGGS are quartz stones rounded by river waters in brazil. The rounded rocks look like the eggs of Emma birds. These stones have been cut and polished on one end.

FOSSIL FERNS have left an imprint of their leaves, called *fronds*, on the rock. They are often found in layers of shale. Ancient ferns first appeared about 395 million years ago.

GARNET is a dark red translucent mineral found embedded in the matrix of igneous or metamorphic rock. Garnet is often cut into gemstones.

GYPSUM is a soft mineral with many commercial uses. It sometimes occurs in rounded shapes called Rosettes or Desert Roses which look like flowers.

Please take descriptive sheet with purchase

SODALITE is colorless in its pure state, but is more commonly found with blue colors. Many specimens are fluorescent in ultraviolet light.

TIGER EYE is a type of quartz which has fibers of asbestos and other minerals trapped inside. Golden brown bands of color shimmer across the surface.

TOURMALINE is a crystal that forms in igneous and metamorphic rocks. It often has striations or grooves. Some types of black tourmaline are used in electrical apparatus.

TURITELLA is a type of gastropod shell. The shell has been fossilized into rock. The coil-shaped cavity of the dead shellfish filled with sediment which later solidified.

ZEBRA ROCK is a type of marble whose impurities segregated into wavy black or grey and white bands due to heat and pressure. The bands look like zebra stripes.

OPTICAL CALCITE is shaped like a rectangle which has been stretched. It is clear and makes lines placed behind it appear double.

PYRITE is a brittle, metallic mineral nicknamed "fool's gold" because its brassy yellow color has fooled a lot of prospectors looking for gold.

QUARTZ is the most common mineral on Earth. It has a hard glassy surface and occurs in many shapes, such as clusters, single points, or solid masses.

ROSE QUARTZ is a type of quartz with a pinkish color probably caused by manganese or titanium. It is popular for jewelry and meditation.

SANDSTONE is a sedimentary rock composed of sand-like crystals of quartz cemented together by silica, lime, or iron oxide. It is found where ancient seas used to exist.

HEMATITE is a dense mineral with metallic luster and a steel-gray color. It is the most important ore of iron.

HOWLITE is a clustered white stone with black markings, found in desert borax deposits. The rounded nodules have been mostly worn smooth by the tumbling process.

JASPER is a type of fine-grained quartz found in earthy reds, yellows, browns and greens. The spotted variety is called bullseye jasper. Some arrowheads are made of jasper.

OBSIDIAN is a type of igneous rock that is like natural glass. Humans have chipped obsidian into arrowheads for hundreds of years. White-spotted obsidian is called snowflake.

OCOS are tiny geodes which are rounded rocks or nodules often found with banded quartz or groupings of crystals inside.

Print-making

1

Mix up the developing chemicals with water of the correct temperature, following the manufacturer's instructions carefully. Choose the negative you would like to print*.

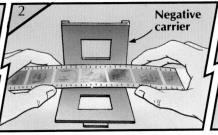

2 Negative carrier

Hold the negative with the shiny side uppermost, and the numbers on the edge furthest from you. Place it in the enlarger negative carrier and slide this into the enlarger.

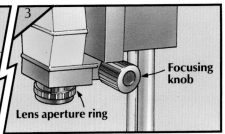

3 Focusing knob / Lens aperture ring

Set the enlarger to the largest aperture. Move the enlarger head to get a correctly sized print. Focus the image; then turn the lens aperture down about two stops.

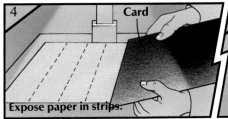

4 Card / Expose paper in strips.

To make a test strip, put some photographic paper on the baseboard, shiny side up. Expose a small strip for five seconds, covering the rest up with black card. Move the card gradually back to expose five further strips, for an extra five seconds each time.

5

Slide the test strip into the developing tray and time it for the recommended period**. Rock the developer tray gently during that time to ensure even development. Do not take the paper out of the developer until the full time is up.

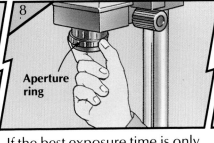

6

Take the paper out of the developer with tongs. Shake off drips and slide it into the stop-bath. Rock the tray gently for a few seconds**. Use another pair of tongs to take the paper out of this tray. Shake off drips and slide the paper into the fixer tray.

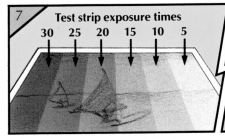

7 Test strip exposure times
30 25 20 15 10 5

After about 30 seconds** rinse the paper in water and look at it in daylight. It will show several contrasting strips, each one representing an exposure time in seconds – 5, 10, 15 etc. Decide which one shows an image which is neither too dark nor too light. Use this exposure time to make your print.

8 Aperture ring

If the best exposure time is only a few seconds, reduce the size of the aperture on the enlarger by a couple of stops, because very short periods are hard to time accurately. If the best exposure is a very long time enlarge the aperture by a couple of stops. In both cases you need another test strip.

9

Under safelight, position some paper, shiny side up, inside the frame on the baseboard. Expose the paper for the correct time, and repeat the processing steps 5-7. Then rinse the print in water for about 20 minutes. Dry fibre-based paper flat on a table. Dry resin-coated paper flat or hang it up.

*If the negative is dusty or marked wipe it with a soft lens cleaning cloth (see page 44).
**Check the manufacturer's instructions on the developing chemicals for specific times.

Printing effects

If you print your own black and white photos there are many things you can do during the process to create special effects. A few are shown below.

Shading, dodging and printing-in

You can alter the tones of a black and white picture during the printing process. If you want to make a particularly dark part of your print lighter you can cover the paper up during part of the *exposure* time by shading or dodging. If you want to make an area of your print darker you can print-in (also called burning-in). These techniques are explained below.

Shading. To lighten a large area of the picture expose the print for part of the correct time, then hold your hand over the area you want lightened for the remaining seconds. Keep it moving gently to blur its edges.

Dodging. Use a dodger to lighten small picture areas. To make a dodger, tape a small piece of white card to a piece of stiff wire. Hold it over the area you want to lighten, keeping it moving gently to blur its edges.

Printing-in. Cut a small hole in some white card. Expose your print for the correct time. Then expose for a while longer, covering the paper with the card. The hole should be over the area you want darker.

Distorting

Try tilting the *enlarger* baseboard in different ways to distort an image. Prop it up with books rather than holding it. For the photo on the right the baseboard was tilted sideways. ▶

Try slipping some holed fabric, such as netting or lace, into the negative holder with the negative. The picture on the right was done using this method. ▶

Photograms

Photograms are photos you can make without a negative. Lay a selection of objects on top of the photographic paper. Choose objects which are fairly flat, with an interesting shape.

Photogram using a piece of fern

Arrange the objects on the paper and switch the light on. Do a test strip to work out the best exposure time. When developed the print should be black except for the areas underneath the objects, as shown above.

Tinting and colouring

◀ You can buy cheap and simple kits to tint black and white prints red, blue or a rich brown colour called sepia, as shown on the left. The kit information will give you detailed instructions.

◀ You can hand-colour prints using special dyes or water-based felt-tip pens, inks or paint. Colour large areas with damp cotton wool dipped in colour. Colour detailed areas with a brush or pen.

Colour processing

When colour *film* is processed and *printed* it takes about 16 different stages to produce a final product. Many people send their colour films to a professional processor for this technically complicated procedure.

Commercial printing

★When a film is sent to a large commercial laboratory it is processed in a machine which takes the film through all the necessary stages mechanically. Once the film is processed the continuous strip of *negatives* is fed through a printing machine.

★ Commercial printing machine controls are set to give a normal, generally acceptable colour level. If there is an unusual colour tone on a picture the machine may filter it out. This can be a problem if the colour tone is deliberate, for instance if you use a special *filter*. Inform the processor that you have used a filter before you have the photo printed. If you notice the fault after the prints are returned explain the problem and get them redone.

Instant picture cameras

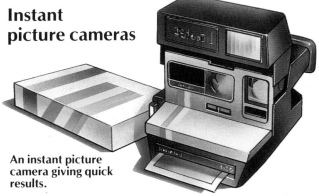

An instant picture camera giving quick results.

Instant picture cameras take a photo that develops and prints itself within minutes. Within the layers of the film there are chemicals which develop and fix the image. Many instant cameras are larger and bulkier than ordinary cameras and the photos which they produce are not always good quality. However, they are easy and fun to use, giving quick results.

Processing faults

There may be occasions when you think the processor is at fault. If you think this is so, take your prints and negatives back and ask for them to be done again. If you use a postal service send them back with a covering note. Take them into a photographic shop first for expert advice if you are unsure. Some examples of processors' mistakes are listed below.

This blob was caused by developer splashed on the negative by the processor.

★ Blobs, uneven colour or hairs. Look carefully at the negative to see if the marks appear. If not get a reprint. If they do ask for your money back.

★ Very light or dark prints. Look at the negative and try to judge if it is normal, or take it into your local photographic shop for advice.

★ Fingerprints on the print. Ask the processor to wipe the fingerprint off the film and redo the print.

★ Scratches on the print. If these appear on the negative it is ruined. If they run parallel down each side this could be due to a camera or film fault. If the scratches are at random angles this could have been done by the processor, so ask for your money back.

★ Out of focus print. Look at your negative through a magnifying glass to see whether the photo was sharp.

Fingerprint

Presenting and storing photos

If you are pleased with the way your pictures have turned out, you will probably want to display them in an album or frame, or put on your own slide show.

On these pages there are lots of tips and hints for displaying and storing your prints and slides. You can also find out how to make your own light box for viewing slides.

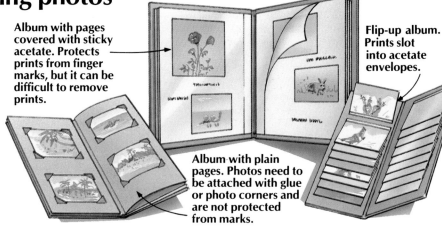

Album with pages covered with sticky acetate. Protects prints from finger marks, but it can be difficult to remove prints.

Flip-up album. Prints slot into acetate envelopes.

Album with plain pages. Photos need to be attached with glue or photo corners and are not protected from marks.

A good way to protect and display your prints is to put them in an album. There are several different types of album available. The main ones are shown above.

Enlargements

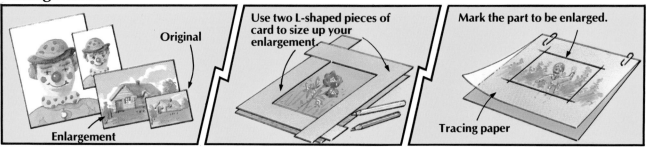

Original

Enlargement

Use two L-shaped pieces of card to size up your enlargement.

Mark the part to be enlarged.

Tracing paper

Your best photos will look more impressive if you have them enlarged. Most processing laboratories can enlarge prints to a variety of standard sizes.

If you particularly like part of a photo, you could have just that section enlarged. You will need to show the laboratory which area is to be enlarged.

Mark the area to be enlarged on some tracing paper clipped over the print, as.shown above. Your enlargement must be the same shape as the original print.

Professional tip

Original   **Cropped photo**

Professional photos are often cropped — any unwanted background is cut away to show only the most important parts and give a dramatic picture. You could crop your own photos before mounting them in an album.

Negatives

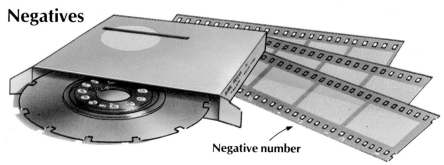

Negative number

Always handle your *negatives* very carefully. Hold them by the edges to avoid marking the image. Protect them from dust and scratches by keeping them in the covers supplied by the processing laboratory.

Negatives are numbered to help you order reprints and enlargements. Give the laboratory the number directly underneath the negative so that they can identify which one you want printed.

Mounting and framing

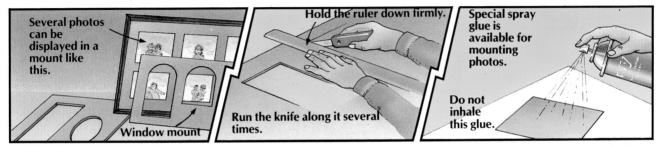

Several photos can be displayed in a mount like this.

Window mount

Hold the ruler down firmly.

Run the knife along it several times.

Special spray glue is available for mounting photos.

Do not inhale this glue.

A good way to display your best prints is to use a frame and a window mount. If your frame does not come with its own mount, you can make one from card with a "window" cut in it.

Measure your frame and work out what size and shape your mount should be. Draw the outline of the mount on the card in pencil. Cut it out with a ruler and craft knife, as shown above.

Stick your photo on a slightly larger piece of backing paper and then lightly glue this to the inside edges of the window mount. Fit the finished mount into the frame.

Slides

If you use slide film, you can display your pictures by using a projector. There is a wide range of projectors available, from hand-operated ones to those that change slides by remote control and focus automatically. Project your slides on to a screen or a white wall.

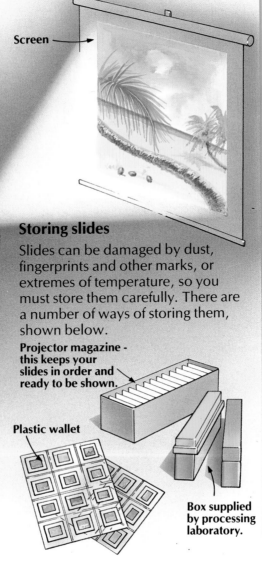

Screen

Projector

Magazine to hold the slides.

Load the slides with the dot in the top right-hand corner, facing the back of the magazine.

Slides have to be loaded into the magazine upside-down and back-to-front. To help load them, it is a good idea to put a dot on the bottom left-hand corner of each slide, as shown above.

Storing slides

Slides can be damaged by dust, fingerprints and other marks, or extremes of temperature, so you must store them carefully. There are a number of ways of storing them, shown below.

Projector magazine - this keeps your slides in order and ready to be shown.

Plastic wallet

Box supplied by processing laboratory.

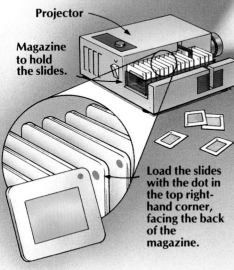

Using a light box

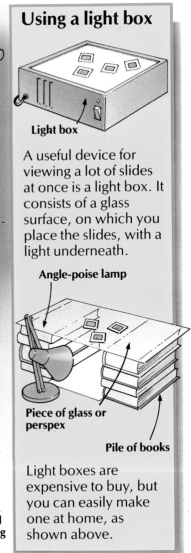

Light box

A useful device for viewing a lot of slides at once is a light box. It consists of a glass surface, on which you place the slides, with a light underneath.

Angle-poise lamp

Piece of glass or perspex

Pile of books

Light boxes are expensive to buy, but you can easily make one at home, as shown above.

Loading and unloading your camera

Disc cameras

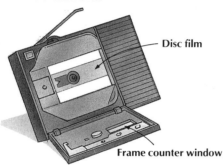

Disc film

Frame counter window

To load the camera, open the *film* compartment door and insert the film. It will only fit in one way. Close the camera door. When you have used all the frames, an "X" will appear in the frame counter window. Open the camera and remove the used disc.

Cartridge-loading cameras (126 and 110)

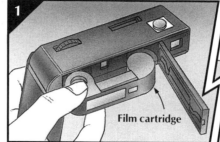

Film cartridge

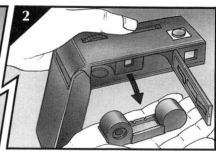

To load the camera, open the film compartment door and insert the film cartridge. It will only fit in one way. Close the door securely. Wind on the film advance until the number "1" appears in the frame counter window – you can then take the first picture.

As you take photos, the number of each frame will appear in the frame counter window. When you have used all the frames, there will be no number in the frame counter window. To unload the camera, open the film compartment door and remove the film cartridge.

35mm and SLR cameras*

Rewind lever

Film cassette

Take-up spool

Film

Open the film compartment door and pull the rewind lever upwards. Insert the film cassette into the film compartment as shown above, with the protruding end at the bottom. Press the rewind lever down to hold the cassette firmly in position.

Gently pull out enough film to insert the end into one of the slots on the take-up spool. Wind on the film and fire the shutter several times until both rows of holes are fitting over the sprockets (teeth). Then shut the film compartment door.

Wind the film on and fire the shutter several times until the number "1" appears in the frame counter window. As you wind on, the film rewind knob should turn in an anti-clockwise direction – this shows that the film is running through correctly.

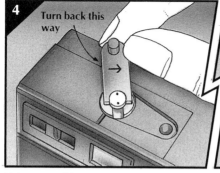

Turn back this way

If the rewind knob does not turn, press the film release stud on the base of the camera, then wind the film rewind knob back half a turn. This winds any unexposed film back into the cassette, so you can open the camera and reload the film.

Rewind lever

Always press the release stud, otherwise you could rip the film.

To unload, press in the film release stud, then turn the rewind lever in a clockwise direction until you feel no more resistance. This winds the film back into the cassette. Open the film compartment door and pull up the rewind lever to release the cassette.

Compact 35mm cameras with "auto-load"

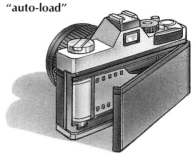

To load, insert the cassette and put the end of the film into the take-up spool, as shown above. Shut the film compartment door – the camera will wind the film on automatically. When all the frames have been used the camera rewinds the film for you.

40   *There are slight variations in loading and unloading some makes of 35mm camera. Refer to your manual if you have problems.*

Focusing and film speeds

A camera needs to be *focused* to get a sharp image (see page 7). There are several different systems for focusing, according to your camera type. You can read about them below.

Focusing symbols

Many 35mm cameras focus using symbols, like the ones shown above, or a series of distances (3m, 1.5m etc) marked on a focusing ring on the barrel of the lens. You should adjust the focusing ring to the appropriate symbol or distance for your picture.

Coupled rangefinder

Unfocused double image

This system is most commonly found on 35mm cameras. If the picture is out of focus, a small area in the centre of the *viewfinder*, called the *rangefinder*, shows a double image. Adjust the focusing ring on the barrel of the lens until the two images merge.

Split-image rangefinder

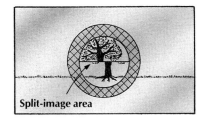

Split-image area

Most *SLR* cameras focus with a split image – the centre of the viewfinder is divided into two semi-circles. The image looks sharp, but if it is out of focus the two halves of the circle are out of alignment. Adjust the focusing ring until the two halves line up.

Autofocus

Subject

Path of pulse

The pulse misses the yacht and makes the camera focus on the background.

Then move camera to compose photo.

Focus camera on main subject!

Automatic cameras send out a pulse of light which bounces off the central subject of the photo. The camera measures how long the pulse takes to return and sets the focus accordingly. Some cameras display the focusing distance in the viewfinder.

If the subject of your photo is not in the centre of the scene, the pulse may pass it by and cause the camera to focus on the background, as shown above. Unwanted foreground objects can also trick the camera, as it will focus on the first object the pulse hits.

Most automatic cameras have a focus lock to overcome this problem. To use the lock, first point the camera at your main subject and press the shutter release half-way down to hold the focus. Then move the camera to compose the scene you want.

Film speeds

There used to be two separate systems for showing *film speeds* : ASA (American Standards Association) and DIN (Deutsche Industrie Norm). To standardize film speeds, one system has now been adopted internationally – the ISO (International Standards Organization) system. An ISO speed consists of the both the ASA and the DIN number, for example ISO 400/ 27°, but on many film packages just the first part of the number (the ASA number) is shown, for example 400 ISO.

The chart on the right will give you some tips on which speed of film to choose for specific conditions. If you will be using the same film in different situations, choose a general purpose speed.

	Colour prints	Colour slides	Black and white
General purpose	100-200	100-200	400
Dull or overcast weather	200-400	200	400
Bright, sunny weather, beach and snow scenes	100-200	25-100	50-125
Sport and action shots	400-1000	400-1000	400-1000
Indoor portraits with natural light	400-1000	400-1000	400-1000
Night scenes	400-1600	400-1000	400-1000
Flash pictures	100-200	100	125
Close-ups	200-400	100-400	125-400
Indoor shots under electric light bulbs	*	400-1000	400-1000

*Special tungsten film for use under electric light bulbs is only available for slides.

Setting the exposure

On many cameras you do not need to set the *exposure* controls (the *shutter speed* and the *aperture*) as the camera does it automatically. However, if you have a manual 35mm or *SLR* camera you will have to set them yourself. On these two pages you can find out about the different exposure systems and how to get the best results from them.

Automatic exposure

Many 110 and compact 35mm cameras set the exposure automatically using an electronic cell on the front of the camera, linked to a built-in *light meter*. This measures how much light there is coming from the overall scene and sets the exposure accordingly. The meter system is powered by a battery, which is usually stored in a compartment on the base of the camera.

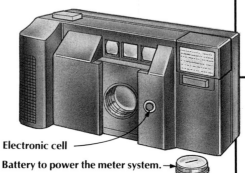

Electronic cell

Battery to power the meter system.

Light subject ends up overexposed.

Automatic meters often set the exposure for the background if there is a strong contrast between the subject and its background. This leaves the subject over or under exposed. This problem can occur in photos such as portraits of people in the snow or on a beach, or people posed in front of windows (dark subjects, light backgrounds), or pictures of brides in white dresses (light subjects, dark backgrounds).

Dark subject ends up underexposed.

If your camera has a film speed dial (see page 9) you can overcome this problem by setting the dial one speed faster for a dark background (to let less light in) or one speed slower for a light background (to let more light in). For example, a film of 200 *ISO* would be set to 400 ISO for a dark background, or 100 ISO for a light background. Some automatic cameras have a special back lighting button to cope with bright backgrounds.

Fixed exposure

Some very simple cameras (such as disc, 110 or 126 cameras) have a pre-set aperture and shutter which cannot be adjusted. The only way to vary the exposure is to use different speeds of film. Some more advanced 110 and 126 cameras have simple aperture controls marked with weather symbols, as shown on the left.

These cameras give their best results in bright, sunny weather. If the weather is dull, it can help to use the *flash,* as this automatically lets more light on to the film.

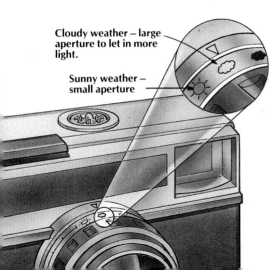

Cloudy weather – large aperture to let in more light.

Sunny weather – small aperture

Manual exposure

Many 35mm and SLR cameras have a manual exposure system – you have to set the shutter speed and/or the aperture. This lets you take pictures in a much wider range of lighting conditions than a camera with automatic exposure and gives you greater control over the appearance of your photos. For example you can blur the background (see page 20), freeze very fast action (see page 28) or take a wide variety of night-time shots (see page 27).

Setting the aperture

Aperture ring

The aperture is normally adjusted using a ring on the barrel of the lens, shown above. This is marked with a series of numbers (such as 5.6, 8, 11), called *f-stops*. The lower the number, the larger the size of the aperture. Opening the aperture wider is often called "opening up", and closing it is called "stopping down".

Bracketing your exposures

If you are in doubt about which exposure to set for a particular picture, it is a good idea to take several pictures using slightly different exposures. This is called *bracketing.*

The best way to do this is to set the first exposure according to the information in your viewfinder, or the suggested exposures on the right. Then take further pictures with the aperture open an extra stop or two, and closed an extra stop or two.

Bracketing your exposures ensures that you end up with at least one acceptable shot of the scene, as well as showing you the wide range of different effects you can achieve by altering the exposure.

Setting the shutter speed

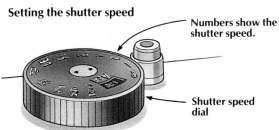

Numbers show the shutter speed.

Shutter speed dial

The shutter speed is normally set using a dial on top of the camera. This is marked with numbers representing fractions of a second – 60 means that the shutter will be open for 1/60th of a second. Many cameras also have a B setting which is used for very long exposures (see page 27).

You should set the shutter speed first. A good general speed is about 1/60th or 1/125th of a second, but difficult conditions may require a faster or slower speed. Think about these factors:

★What is the light like? If it is very bright, choose a fast shutter speed so that the film is not overexposed. If the conditions are dark, you need a slow shutter speed to let enough light in.

★Is your subject still or moving? In an action shot you need a fast shutter speed to freeze the movement. For a still-life a slow shutter speed is best.

★How long can you hold the camera still? If you are hand-holding a heavy camera, or using a large extra lens (such as a *telephoto*), you will need a fast shutter speed to avoid camera shake.

The needle should be in the middle of the frame for a correct aperture.

Green light comes on when the aperture is correct.

Information inside film box

Aperture controls on 35mm cameras give you great control over your photos.

The aperture is set according to the lighting conditions: in sunlight you need a small aperture, in dull weather a larger one. Many cameras help you to select a suitable aperture for the shutter speed you have set by displaying information in the *viewfinder*. Two common systems for doing this are shown above.

If your camera does not have aperture information in the viewfinder, you have to work out both the shutter speed and the aperture size yourself. To help you, suggested exposures for various conditions are shown in the chart below. There is often an exposure guide printed on the inside of film boxes, which can also be useful.

On a manual camera, altering the size of the aperture helps you to cope with a strong contrast between the subject and the background (this problem is explained on the previous page). If you think the camera may underexpose the subject, open the aperture by an extra stop. If it may overexpose, close the aperture by one stop.

Suggested exposures

	100 ISO	200 ISO	400 ISO
Bright sun on sand or snow	1/125 f22	1/250 f22	1/500 f22
Bright sun	1/125 f16	1/250 f16	1/500 f16
Weak or hazy sun	1/125 f11	1/250 f11	1/500 f11
Cloudy and bright	1/125 f8	1/250 f8	1/500 f8
Cloudy and dull	1/125 f5.6	1/250 f5.6	1/500 f5.6
Shade	1/125 f5.6	1/250 f5.6	1/500 f5.6

Aperture and shutter priority cameras

Some 35mm and SLR cameras have semi-automatic exposure – you set one control and the camera sets the other one. With a shutter priority camera, you set the shutter and the camera sets the aperture. Aperture priority cameras work the other way round.

Suggested exposures for night-time shots

	400 ISO
Dusk shots	1/60 f2.8
Shop window and neon signs	1/60 f2.8
Street lights	1/15 f2.8
Floodlit buildings	1/8 f2.8
Candle light	1/4 f2.8
Car light trails	10 secs f22
Fireworks	3-4 secs f11

Suggested shutter speeds* for action shots

	100 ISO
Person walking	1/125
Person running	1/500
Cyclist	1/250-1/1000
Galloping horse	1/250-1/1000
Sports (football, tennis etc)	1/500
Car, train etc	1/250-1/1000

*You will need to set the aperture according to the individual lighting conditions.

Useful accessories

Your camera will last for years if it is looked after well. To keep it working properly, you should protect it from knocks and scratches and keep it clean. On these two pages you can find out about protecting and cleaning your camera and about some extra photographic equipment.

Protecting your camera

The equipment shown below will protect your camera from knocks and prevent dust and grit from getting inside the camera.

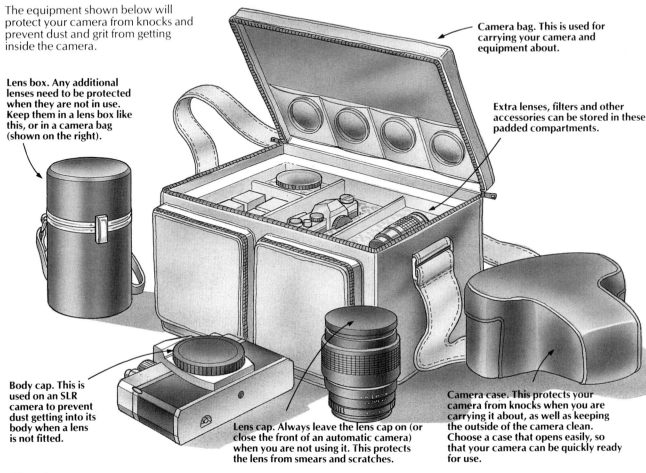

Lens box. Any additional lenses need to be protected when they are not in use. Keep them in a lens box like this, or in a camera bag (shown on the right).

Camera bag. This is used for carrying your camera and equipment about.

Extra lenses, filters and other accessories can be stored in these padded compartments.

Body cap. This is used on an SLR camera to prevent dust getting into its body when a lens is not fitted.

Lens cap. Always leave the lens cap on (or close the front of an automatic camera) when you are not using it. This protects the lens from smears and scratches.

Camera case. This protects your camera from knocks when you are carrying it about, as well as keeping the outside of the camera clean. Choose a case that opens easily, so that your camera can be quickly ready for use.

Cleaning your camera

It is a good idea to clean your camera and lenses regularly to prevent damage from dust, grit or moisture. Be very gentle, particularly when cleaning the inside of your camera. Try to avoid touching the *shutter,* or the mirror on an SLR camera, as it is very easy to damage these delicate parts. Some useful equipment for cleaning your camera is shown on the right.

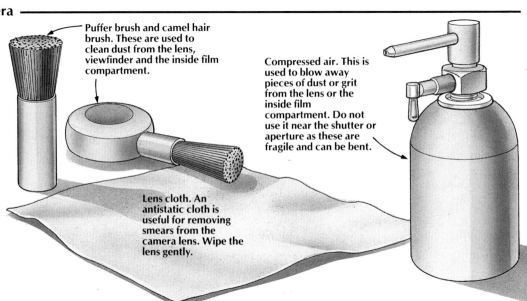

Puffer brush and camel hair brush. These are used to clean dust from the lens, viewfinder and the inside film compartment.

Compressed air. This is used to blow away pieces of dust or grit from the lens or the inside film compartment. Do not use it near the shutter or aperture as these are fragile and can be bent.

Lens cloth. An antistatic cloth is useful for removing smears from the camera lens. Wipe the lens gently.

Tripods

A *tripod* is particularly useful for long *exposures* (such as night-time shots) when camera shake can easily spoil your pictures. Most tripods have adjustable legs and an adjustable head to support the camera in different positions.

If you do not want to carry a full-sized tripod around with you, useful alternatives are a mini tripod, which can stand on any surface, or a camera clamp, which can be attached to a branch, post or railings.

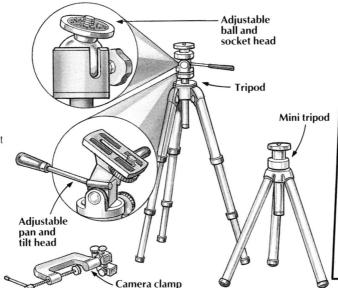

Adjustable ball and socket head

Tripod

Mini tripod

Adjustable pan and tilt head

Camera clamp

Features to look for:

★ Sturdiness. The tripod should be as heavy as you can carry. The heavier it is, the less the risk of camera shake. Set the tripod up and shake it to see how firm it is.

★ Type of head. A ball and socket head is usually cheaper, but a pan and tilt head is easier to adjust.

★ Type of feet. Spiked feet are useful for holding the tripod down outdoors, but will be useless for indoor work.

★ Adjustability. Look for a tripod that can be set to a wide variety of different heights. Some tripods cannot be set to very low levels.

Light meter

Most cameras have a built-in *light meter* to help you set the exposure, but a hand-held light meter can still be useful. Most built-in meters take a general reading from the whole scene. A hand-held meter can measure the amount of light being reflected from the actual subject, allowing you to set a very accurate exposure.

Features to look for:

★ How sensitive is it? Cheap selenium meters often do not work well in low light levels. Cadmium sulphide (CdS) meters use a cell that is many times more sensitive to light.

★ Ease of use. Are the dials easy to read?

Hand-held light meter

Motor drive

A *motor drive* winds on the film after each shot, and is used to take a lot of pictures in quick succession – for example of a moving subject or at a sports event.

Some cameras have a slower type of motor drive (called an auto-winder) built in. A separate motor drive can be fitted to an SLR camera, as shown below. This lets you take between two and six pictures per second, but the unit can also be set to fire single frames.

Features to look for:

★ How fast can it take pictures? Look for the number of frames it can take each second.

★ Does it have automatic rewind to help you change films quickly?

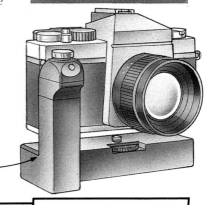

A motor drive fits on to the bottom of the camera.

Batteries

Built-in light meters, automatic cameras, motor drives and separate *flash* units are all powered by batteries. These need replacing regularly – when indicated by the camera's battery test button, or, for a flash, when the "flash ready" light takes longer than usual to come on. It is a good idea to find out what size of battery your camera uses and to keep a spare set.

Feature to look for:

★ If possible, choose a camera with a battery test button. This enables you to check that the batteries are not flat.

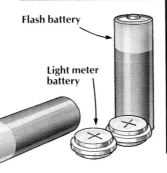

Flash battery

Light meter battery

Cable release

It is easy to jog the camera when you press the shutter release. To prevent this, it is a good idea to use a *cable release*. This allows you to fire the shutter without touching the camera.

Features to look for:

★ A long and flexible cable is best.

★ Buy a cable with a locking device if you want to take very long exposures.

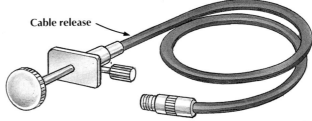

Cable release

Glossary

Angle of view. The amount of a scene that a camera can fit into a photo. This varies with different lens types.

Aperture. A hole next to the camera lens, surrounded by a circle of moveable metal blades. The hole size can be enlarged or reduced to vary the amount of light that can pass through it on to the film.

ASA. Initials standing for the American Standards Association. A system of showing film speeds.

Autofocus. An automatic focusing system, which bounces a beam of infra-red light off a subject in front of the camera lens, measuring its distance from the camera. The camera focus is then automatically adjusted.

Bellows unit. An extension which can be fitted between a lens and a camera body. Its length can be extended or reduced to vary the focusing distance of the camera, so that it can focus on close-up subjects.

Bracketing. Taking several shots of the same subject using different exposure settings, in order to be sure of getting at least one correct exposure.

Cable release. An extension cable which can be connected to the shutter release button on a camera. A switch on the end of the cable allows you to take a picture without touching your camera, avoiding camera shake.

Close-up lens. A lens which enables a camera to focus on close-up subjects. It can be mounted in front of an ordinary camera lens.

Composition. The arrangement of objects or elements which appear in a picture.

Darkroom. A light-tight room used when developing and printing film.

Depth of field. The distance in a photograph from the nearest point that is in focus to the furthest point away that is still in focus.

Developing. The process of making an image appear on film or on photographic paper.

Diffuser. Translucent material, such as fabric or tracing paper, placed in front of a light source. It has the effect of spreading out the light and softening its effect.

DIN. Initials standing for Deutsche Industrie Norm. A system of showing film-speeds.

DX coding. A pattern of metallic squares on a 35mm film cassette case, which some cameras can read to enable them to set the film speed.

Enlarger. A vertically mounted projector, which is used to enlarge negatives and project them on to photographic paper to print a picture.

Exposure. The total amount of light that reaches the film in a camera. This is controlled by the brightness of the subject, the shutter speed and the size of the aperture.

Extension tube. A tube which fits between the lens and the body of a camera, to allow the camera to focus on close-up objects.

Fill-in flash. Using flash outdoors to soften shadows cast by strong sunlight.

Film. A flexible transparent base with a coating which reacts to light, and which is used to record a photographic image.

Film speed. A measurement used to describe how quickly or slowly a film reacts to light.

Filter. A tinted glass or plastic disc or square, which fits on to a camera lens. A filter alters the way that light affects film, for instance to enhance colour or achieve an unusual effect.

Fixing. The third stage of film development, which dissolves away undeveloped silver particles to make an image insensitive to light.

Flash. An instrument which creates an artificial burst of light, to illuminate a dark scene so that an image can be recorded on film.

Focal length. A lens measurement – the distance needed between a camera lens and the film in order for a distant object to be sharply focused.

Focusing. Making an image appear sharply on a film by moving the camera lens backwards or forwards.

F-stop. The size of a camera aperture is measured in numbers called f-stops. The smaller the f-stop number, the larger the aperture.

Hot shoe. A clip on the top of a 35mm camera for attaching a separate flash unit.

ISO. Initials standing for International Standards Organization. A system of showing film speeds.

Lens. A curved glass or plastic disc which bends light rays coming into the camera, so that they form an image on the film.

Light meter. A mechanism for measuring the amount of light coming from a subject.

Macro lens. A lens which can be used to focus on very close-up shots, or for normal photography. It can be fitted on to cameras which have detachable ordinary lenses.

Motor drive. An electric motor which winds a film on automatically, and then triggers the camera shutter release to take another picture. Motor drives normally take 4-6 frames a second. A slower version is called an autowind (2-4 frames a second).

Negative. A photographic image on film, where the normal tones are reversed – the light parts of a scene appear dark and the dark parts appear transparent.

Parallax error. The difference between the image which you see through a viewfinder and the image which reaches the film through the camera lens. This does not occur on SLR cameras, which have single reflex viewfinding systems.

Printing. The process of transferring an image from film on to light-sensitive paper.

Rangefinder. A focusing aid used on 35mm cameras. A double image or a split image is shown in the viewfinder until the camera is properly focused, when only one image appears.

Safelight. A working light used when printing photos in a darkroom. It emits coloured light, usually red or orange, which does not affect photographic paper.

Self-timer. A camera mechanism which operates a camera shutter automatically after about ten seconds delay, to enable the photographer to move in front of the camera and appear in the picture.

Shutter. A barrier positioned behind the camera lens. When a picture is taken it opens to let light through. The speed at which it opens and shuts helps to control the amount of light allowed on to the film.

Single lens reflex camera (SLR). A camera with a built-in mirror system which enables viewing and focusing to be carried out through the camera lens itself, instead of through a separate viewfinder. This eliminates any differences between the viewfinder and lens views.

Stop-bath. A chemical which is used to halt the action of developer during the process of developing a film or a print.

Telephoto lens. A lens which makes objects appear closer than they really are.

Tripod. A camera support with three legs, which can be adjusted to different heights. A camera can be attached to the tripod head.

Viewfinder. A camera window you can look through to compose a picture before taking a shot.

Wide-angle lens. A lens which has a wider angle of view than an ordinary lens.

Zoom lens. A lens which has an adjustable focal length, so that its effect can be varied.

Index

Acknowledgements

Windsurfing photo on the cover
courtesy of Astonocean Photo Library.

Additional photos courtesy of Allsports,
Art Directors and Spectrum photo
libraries.